Practical Design & Technology

Electronic Constructions

Steven Atkin & Richard Beeden

Heinemann
LIBRARY

www.heinemann.co.uk/library

Visit our website to find out more information about **Heinemann Library** books.

To order:

☎ Phone 44 (0) 1865 888066

▤ Send a fax to 44 (0) 1865 314091

▭ Visit the Heinemann Bookshop at www.heinemann.co.uk/library to browse our catalogue and order online.

First published in Great Britain by Heinemann Library, Halley Court, Jordan Hill, Oxford OX2 8EJ, part of Harcourt Education. Heinemann is a registered trademark of Harcourt Education Ltd.

Editorial: Andrew Farrow, Lucy Thunder and Helen Cox
Design: David Poole and Paul Myerscough
Illustrations: Kamaedesign
Picture Research: Catherine Bevan and Rebecca Sodergren
Production: Séverine Ribierre

Originated by Ambassador Litho Ltd
Printed in Hong Kong, China by Wing King Tong

ISBN 0 431 17580 2
07 06 05 04 03
10 9 8 7 6 5 4 3 2 1

British Library Cataloguing in Publication Data
Atkin, Steven and Beeden, Richard
Electronic Constructions. – (Practical Design and Technology)
621.3'81
A full catalogue record for this book is available from the British Library.

Acknowledgements
The publishers would like to thank the following for permission to reproduce photographs:
Corbis/Royalty p.**18**; Gareth Boden pp. **10b**, **22**, **26a**, **26c**, **26d**, **28**, **31a**, **31c**, **31d**, **31e**, **32**, **34a**, **35c**, **35d**, **36a**, **36b**, **39a**, **39b**, **40a**, **43b**, **43d**, **44**, **45**; Bridgeman Photo Library p.**14**; Economatics pp. **40b**, **41**, **41b**, **43a**; Mega Electronics pp. **12**, **13**, **25a**; Nintendo p. **16b**; Nokia p. **15**; Photodisc p. **4**; Sony p. **16a**; Suregrave p. **25b**; Tudor Photography pp. **6**, **10a**, **38**, **39c**, **43c**.

Cover photograph of the circuit board and PICBU robot, reproduced with permission of Gareth Boden.

The publishers would like to thank Andy Bird for his assistance in the preparation of this book, the staff and pupils of both Hope Valley College, Derbyshire and Wales High School, Rotherham, AME Product Development Solutions and Mega Electronics. Also, thanks to Economatics (Education) Ltd for their assistance with the PICBU project.

Every effort has been made to contact copyright holders of any material reproduced in this book. Any omissions will be rectified in subsequent printings if notice is given to the publishers.

Contents

Any words appearing in the text in bold, **like this,** are explained in the Glossary.

Electronics

Electronics is one of the fastest growing and most exciting fields of technology. This book provides an introduction to some areas of the world of electronic engineering.

The book looks at electronic projects that you could design and make either at school or at home. The projects are broken down into small stages so you can follow them easily. The book explains areas of design technology project work that are needed for the design and manufacturing process, such as product **analysis**, design **specifications** and product **evaluation**.

What are electronic products?

Electronic products use the energy of electricity to make them work. Lightning is nature's greatest display of electricity in action. Fortunately we do not require that much electrical energy to make electronic projects work!

Electronic products use a number of different electronic **components** fixed to a printed circuit board (PCB). The components are connected by copper tracks. Each component performs a different job. With the electronic components in place, the electronic **circuit** converts electrical energy into a useful product.

The lightning seen in the sky is electricity in action in nature.

Why electronics are used

Electronics allow products to do jobs quickly and cheaply. Scientists and inventors have created lots of electrical devices and gadgets to make our lives easier and more entertaining. Electronics are constantly being developed. As technology advances, so electronic components get smaller and work faster. As they get smaller they usually get cheaper to manufacture, which brings the cost of electrical goods down. Some examples of everyday products using electronic components are the personal computer, television, washing machine, microwave oven and mobile phone.

The basics about electricity

What is electricity? Everything is made of very small particles called **atoms**. Atoms are made of **protons, electrons** and **neutrons**. The discovery of the electron, a part of the atom, helped scientists to explain how electricity worked.

Electrons can move at high speed through **conductive materials** such as metals, gases, moist air and a **vacuum**, or they can rest still on a surface. Electrons, however, can not travel through **insulating materials** such as glass, plastic, rubber and wood. A stream of moving electrons is called an electrical **current**. It is the movement of millions and millions of microscopic electrons through a conductive material that creates electric current – electricity.

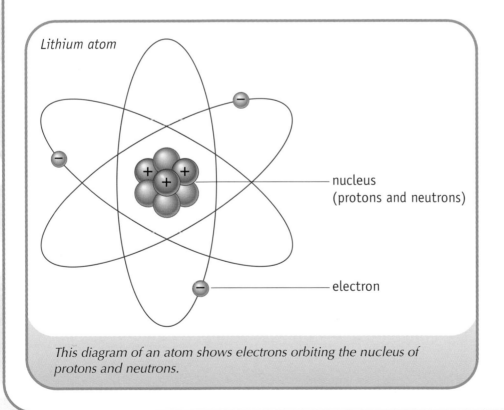

Lithium atom

nucleus
(protons and neutrons)

electron

This diagram of an atom shows electrons orbiting the nucleus of protons and neutrons.

The design process

The task of designing and making something is very complicated. The designer needs to think about a wide range of things, from the materials that could be used, to the requirements of the **consumer**. The whole activity is often described as the 'design process'. The design process is a framework for designing and making, and is used by designers all over the world in the design and manufacture of a wide range of products. This book will look at the design process for designing and making electronic products, that is products that are designed and manufactured using electronic **components**. The design process has nine basic stages and is as follows:

Stage 1

Identifying an area of need or opportunity – this is where a company, designer or individual identifies a problem with an existing product, or sees an opportunity to develop a new product.

Stage 2

Developing a **design brief** – this is a statement that describes the problem that needs to be solved.

Stage 3

Research – this involves finding out as much information about the design brief as possible. There are many different areas of research, but the main ones in electronic products are:

- Electricity – it is important to understand the various terms used to describe the properties of electricity
- Components – finding out what components could be used in the design
- Materials and equipment – finding out about the different materials, machines and processes that could be used in manufacturing the product
- Product analysis – this is looking at existing products and thinking about how they can help in the design of a product
- Users – finding out what people want from the product

Stage 4

Design specification – this is the development of a precise description of what the product must have and do. It is often separated into a user **specification** (what it must do to satisfy the people who want it) and a manufacturing specification (how it will be made and to what quality).

Looking at the inside of a mobile phone is a form of product analysis.

Stage 5

Design ideas – this is the generation of a number of ideas that meet the requirements of the design specification. They are usually done by hand initially, but they can also be developed using Computer Aided Design (CAD) programs such as Adobe Illustrator®.

Stage 6

Product development – this is the process of getting from a number of design ideas to the point at which the designer is ready to manufacture the **prototype**. This involves **modelling** different ways of making the product, and the production of working drawings and manufacturing instructions.

Stage 7

Planning – this is the accurate planning of how to make the final product. It is sometimes done in the form of a **flowsheet**, with different symbols used to represent different stages of the making process.

Stage 9

Testing and **evaluation** – evaluating means thinking about how well the project has gone. It is important that the product is tested to check that it meets the design specification. It can be broken down into three main questions:

1. What have I done well?
2. What could I have done better?
3. How could I improve the finished product?

Stage 8

Manufacturing – this is the making of a product.

! Health and safety

Take care and work safely.

Eye protection

Wear eye protection when soldering circuits. Goggles or spectacles should be approved to British Standard 2092 and/or EN166 or international equivalent.

Solder

Rosin-free solder is now available and recommended for educational use. It is designed to reduce asthma, which can be triggered by rosin use.

UV lightboxes

Photosensitive printed circuit boards need to be exposed to ultraviolet (UV) light. UV lightboxes provide the UV light, but UV light can damage eyesight. Close UV boxes before switching them on.

Current

Electrical **current** can flow in either of two directions. If it always flows in one direction it is called direct current (DC). A battery provides a safe, steady DC voltage, ranging from 1.5 to 9 volts (V). Electronic projects should never need more than 30V. The plug sockets in your home provide a constantly changing voltage. This is called alternating current (AC). The mains voltage in the UK is 240V (Australia 220V) and dangerous. You cannot use mains electricity for electronic projects. They will not work, and you may be killed. Always use an approved, correctly fused plug with any electrical appliance. If uncertain, use a certified **circuit** breaker or consult a qualified electrician.

Understanding electricity

Research lets you find out what has been done before. It gives you greater knowledge and understanding of something. It lets you find out what works and what does not. Without research you will find it difficult to form design ideas and move your project work forward.

The first step in project research in electronics is to understand what makes electrical or electronic devices work.

Understanding electric current

An electric **current** is a stream of moving **electrons**. Electrons carry electric current or charge. The higher the current, the greater the flow of electrons. Current is measured in amperes, or 'amps', shown by the symbol A, for example 3A is 3 amps. Some very small currents are measured in milliamperes. For example, 1000 mA = 1 amp.

Understanding voltage

Voltage is electrical force. If electricity is compared to water flowing through a pipe, voltage is the pressure that pushes the electricity around a **circuit**. A battery will provide this push or force and make electrons move. This force is also known as the **electromotive force** (**EMF**). A chemical reaction inside the battery will push electrons out of the negative terminal and around to the positive terminal of the battery. There must be a **conductive material** between the two terminals for this to happen. Voltage is sometimes called potential difference. It is measured in volts, shown by the symbol V, for example 6V is 6 volts. The higher the voltage, the more energy each electron has to spend as it travels around a circuit.

Understanding power

Power is the rate of work done per second by an electrical current, or the amount of energy transformed per second. It equals work done divided by time taken. If work done (energy) is measured in joules, one joule (J) per second is called a watt. Power is measured in watts (W) or kilowatts (kW), 1 kW = 1000 W. Power rating is calculated by multiplying the current flowing by the voltage across a **component**.

Power (W) = current (I) x voltage (V)

Understanding energy

Energy is measured in joules, shown by the symbol J. Most appliances get their energy from the mains (plug sockets).

A hairdryer changes electrical energy into heat to dry your hair – energy cannot be destroyed, only changed into different forms. The higher the power rating, the quicker the appliance will take energy from the mains.

Appliances usually have a power rating marked on them in watts or kilowatts –
for example, a hairdryer (1800W) or iron (1200W). Electricity supply companies
measure energy in kilowatt-hours (kWh), the commercial unit of electrical energy.

Energy (kWh) = power (kW) x time (in hours)

Understanding resistance

Resistance is found in conductive
materials. Resistance is measured
in ohms (Ω). Some conductors
will resist the flow of electric
current more than others.
Resistance has the effect of
slowing down the flow of electric
current. The more resistance
there is in a circuit, the lower
the current.

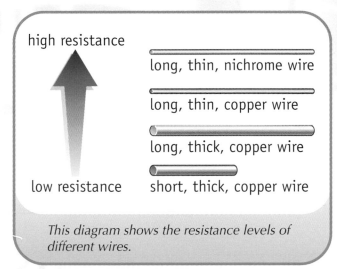

This diagram shows the resistance levels of
different wires.

Which way does the current flow?

Electrical current can flow in either of two directions through a conductor. If it always
flows in just one direction it is called direct current or DC. A battery provides DC. In
your home, the plug sockets in the wall provide a constantly changing voltage. This is
called alternating current, or AC, in which the electrons move backwards and forwards
in the circuit. The mains voltage in houses in the UK is 240V (Australia 220V).

Units in electronics

Unit	Abbreviation	Measured in (symbol)	Equivalents	Formula (ohms law)
Current	I	amperes (A)	1A=1000mA	I=V/R
Voltage (potential difference)	V	volts (V)		V=IR
Resistance	R	ohms (Ω)	1kΩ=1000Ω	R=V/I
Power	P	watts (W)	1kW=1000W	P=VxI
Energy	J	joules (J)	1kJ=1000J	E=Pxt

Investigating electronic components

Here are some of the many different electronic **components** you could use in your projects. See pages 44–45 for **specifications** of a further range of components.

A light dependent resistor, which senses light levels.

Sensors

Sensors are devices that can detect changes in heat, light, moisture, radiation, movement or sound. Sensors are input components, which means they provide information. A sensor works by detecting when the voltage level in a **circuit** changes.

A moisture sensor will sense when moisture is present or not present. A moisture sensor can be connected in two ways:

- Sensor Wet, which indicates when moisture is sensed – for example, a water level detector will tell when a bath is full.
- Sensor Dry, which indicates when moisture is not sensed – for example, a soil tester will tell when the soil is dry in a plant pot.

Transistors

A transistor is an electronic switch. It can also be used as an **amplifier**. Transistors have three legs. A small **current** at one leg, called the base, can control a much larger current flowing through the other two legs, which are called the collector and emitter.

Transistors are made from three material layers; each layer has a leg:

- (C) Collector leg – this leg collects current from an **output** device, for example, a light emitting diode (LED)
- (B) Base leg – current flows into the base of this leg, which acts like a trigger
- (E) Emitter leg – this leg emits amplified current to the **negative power rail**.

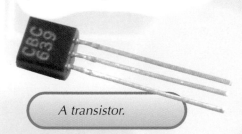

A transistor.

Resistors

Resistors are used to reduce the flow of electric current through a circuit. Resistors usually have coloured bands, called a colour code, that represent the resistor value, for example 1000 ohms.

A voltage of from 0.6V to 0.8V between the base leg and the emitter leg is required to switch on a transistor.

Imagine a wet/dry sensor in the ground. When the soil moisture level decreases, the resistance across the sensor will increase. As a result, the voltage across the sensor will rise, increasing the current that will flow into the base leg of the transistor. If the voltage rises above 0.6 volts, the transistor will switch on. This will allow current to flow between the collector leg and the emitter leg. This current flow will in turn activate an output device such as an LED (see below).

Diodes

A diode conducts electricity in one direction only. It acts like an electronic one-way valve. A diode will only conduct current when the forward voltage reaches a certain level – 0.6 volts or more.

A light emitting diode, or LED, is a small light that glows when small amounts of electric current flow through it. An LED can be used to show when a product is on or off, or as an alert. A resistor is needed with an LED, to make sure the amount of current is very small.

Thyristors

Thyristors are **solid state** switches. They will not amplify **fluctuating** signals like a transistor. Thyristors have three legs called the anode, cathode and gate. Like a diode, a thyristor will only allow current to flow in one direction. It will only allow current to flow if a small current is allowed to flow through the gate leg. Any current, however small or flowing for a short time, will switch the thyristor on. The thyristor will then stay on until it is reset. In other words it is 'latched'.

Capacitors

A **capacitor** is a device that stores electrical charge. It is made of two tiny plates, which can conduct electricity. These plates are separated by a thin layer of an insulator, usually a plastic. In the projects in this book, a capacitor is used to store a small amount of charge and then release it like a tiny rechargeable battery.

Transducer

Transducers convert an input energy into a different kind of energy. There are many types of transducer. For example, an electroacoustic transducer can convert electrical signals into sound, such as in a buzzer or loudspeaker. A **piezo-electric transducer** converts electricity into movement, such as in a strain gauge.

Investigating an integrated circuit

An **integrated circuit (IC)** is a collection of individual components (such as transistors, resistors, capacitors and diodes). These are formed on a tiny wafer chip of **silicon**. The components are connected by aluminium wires on the surface of the chip. Many different integrated circuits exist and all perform different jobs. They have made possible video games, computers and other sophisticated products.

Materials and equipment

Here are some of the many different materials and equipment you could use in your projects.

Printed circuit boards

Printed **circuit** boards (PCBs) are made from a thin sheet of copper **laminated** to a base. The base can be made from epoxy glass fibre or cheaper or softer laminates. PCBs can be plain copper on laminate, or **photosensitive**. The copper of photosensitive boards is coated with a layer that reacts to ultraviolet light. Photosensitive boards are protected by a black plastic film. Plain PCBs can be used with **etch** resistant transfers, pens and for **CNC milling**; they cannot be used with ultraviolet light. The copper layer is removed by etching or milling to leave **circuit** connections.

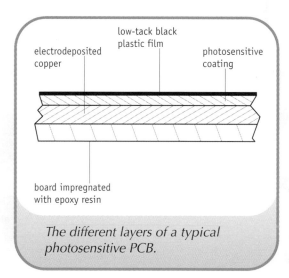

The different layers of a typical photosensitive PCB.

Ultraviolet lightboxes

Photosensitive PCBs need to be exposed to ultraviolet (UV) light to expose the PCB design. UV lightboxes provide a UV illuminated area on which to expose PCB boards. Remember that UV light can damage people's eyesight, so the box must be closed before being switched on. Once exposed, the PCB is exposed to a developing solution, which will ensure that only the copper that has been exposed to UV light will be removed by the etching process.

PCB processing tanks

PCB processing tanks can perform a number of operations. They can develop UV exposed boards in developing solution, etch the copper from PCBs using ferric chloride chemicals or heated **fine etch crystals**; or tin plate an etched circuit. A different tank is needed for each operation.

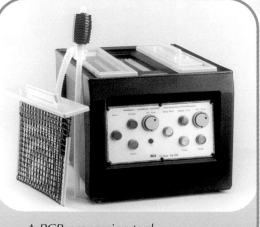

A PCB processing tank.

PCB drill

PCB drills are vertically mounted high-speed power drills. They are used for drilling 1mm diameter holes through PCBs to allow **components** to be soldered to them.

Soldering iron

Soldering irons provide a heat source of up to 340°C. This will melt solder and allow the legs of components to be fixed to the copper track of a PCB.

Solder wire

There are a number of different types of solder wire, usually known as solder. Solder is composed of a tin/lead alloy and contains a core material of flux. Flux acts to clean and help the metals join. Solder generally melts between 180°C and 248°C depending on which type is used. **Rosin**-free solder is now available and recommended for educational use. Although it is more expensive than ordinary solder it is designed to reduce the likelihood of asthma, which can be triggered by rosin use.

A PCB drill with a 1 mm drill bit (for drilling 1 mm holes).

Solder wire.

Product analysis

What product analysis involves

Product **analysis** is where designers look at an existing product that is similar to the one they want to make. We will look at it in a lot of detail as part of designers' research and it will help us to design ideas in the future.

Product analysis involves looking at things (observing) and thinking about them (analysing).

In the course of researching a project you will collect pictures and research data on existing similar products. You should examine the information you find in detail. This can give you valuable insights into how methods and materials are best used. Good design brings together and uses a lot of information. You will need to develop skills to solve each 'design and make' problem as you come across it.

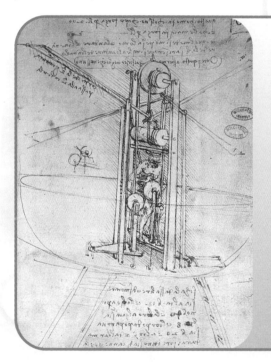

Leonardo da Vinci was a famous artist, scientist and designer. He designed a parachute and painted the famous Mona Lisa. Leonardo da Vinci was one of the first people to realize how important product analysis was. Leonardo learned a lot about things by observation and analysis. This picture shows his sketch for a flying machine!

Product analysis for a electronic product

A product analysis has a few small steps:

1. Look carefully at the electronic product you wish to analyse. Sketch it from various angles (above, side on, beneath). Alternatively, use pictures or photographs of it.

2. Next add comments about what you see. Make notes with arrows pointing to the part of the product it is related to. This is called annotation.

Use the different headings within the tables on the next page to create a table of your own, describing the product. Each heading is about a characteristic of the product you are analysing. On the picture or sketch you have made of the product, ask and answer questions about each characteristic of the product.

Analysing the outer casing

Casing material	Materials can be soft, hard, durable (hard wearing), strong, water resistant, weak, flexible, heavy, light. What material is the outer casing made of?
Manufacture of casing	How has it been manufactured?
Fixing of casing	How many parts is it in? If more than one, how are they fitted together?
Shape	2D objects have shape (such as triangle or circle). 3D objects have form (like a pyramid or sphere). What is the shape of the casing like? Is it smooth or angular, for example?
Decoration of casing	Any patterns or shapes or pictures?
Texture and colouring of casing	Texture is the way a surface feels (smooth, rough, hard, soft, gooey). Is the casing rough or smooth, clear or coloured?

You could try analysing a product, like this mobile phone, for yourself.

Inside the electronic product

Inputs	What are the inputs into the product? Are they buttons or switches?
Process	What makes the product work? Does the product use an **integrated circuit (IC)**? Is it identifiable by a number? Does it use more than one IC?
Components	What other **components** can be seen?
Outputs	What **outputs** does the product use? Light, sound, movement?
Power	How is it powered? What type of battery does it use?
Construction	How is the PCB fitted into the casing?

Design specifications explained

What does a specification do?

A design **specification** describes in simple sentences what you intend your product to be like and what you hope to achieve. It should be very easy to read. For example, you could use bullet points to keep it neat and easy to read.

When do I do a specification?

A specification is done after you have completed your project research and product **analysis**, but before you write down your initial design ideas.

Both of these products perform the same function, as electronic games, but the product design is very different.

Why do I need a specification?

A specification sets out the targets, called criteria, that you have identified for your project. The targets need to be clear and easily understood by other people. When you **evaluate** your product you will need to refer to the specification to see if the final outcome meets the targets set out in the original specification.

What does a specification look like?

A specification is best presented as a series or table of bullet-pointed statements or **criteria**. The statements can be open or fixed in nature. Do not write a descriptive paragraph like a story, though.

What type of statement should I use?

Specification statements can be fixed, semi-fixed or open in nature. An example of each would be:

- Open statement – My product can be any colour.
- Semi-fixed statement – My product will be a bright primary colour.
- Fixed statement – My product will be the colour red.

The specification below is for a child's chair. Specification statements will be required for the following criteria:

Criteria	Example statement
Main function	My product will seat a three-year-old child comfortably.
Other functions	My product will act as a rocking chair.
Size	My product will be small in size.
Weight	My product should be as light as possible.
Durability	My product should withstand regular usage.
Materials	My product will be made from a combination of materials.
Appearance/shape	My product will be appealing to young children.
Style/form	My product will be in the form of a animal.
Colour/texture	My product will use a range of smooth gloss colours.
Market	My product is aimed at the infant market.
Manufacturing cost	My product will cost approximately £5 ($A13) to make.
Selling price	My product will sell for about £15 ($A39).
Maintenance	My product will be maintenance free.
Safety	My product will have no sharp edges or small parts.
Where it is used	My product will be able to be used indoors.
Construction time	My product will be made in 16 workshop hours.
Environmental issues	My product will use an economical amount of material.
Manufacturing	My product should lend itself to mass production.
Quality	My product will be high quality.

Designing for electronics

The easiest way to approach designing electronics is to break the process down into easy parts. This is known as a **systems approach**. An electronic product will have three blocks to it:

Input → process → output

- The input enters information into the system. It will normally contain a switch or a sensor of some kind.

- The process receives information from the input and uses it to control the output.

- The **output** gives out information or makes things happen. Output **components** usually light up, move or make a sound to show the user what is happening.

The Internet is a good source of information at the research and development stage of a design.

Developing a design

Imagine that you have decided that you want to know when to water plants in a house. To do this you will need to design and make an electronic device that can sense changes in moisture levels, to tell you when a plant needs watering. Before the electronic device can be made you will need more information and knowledge. You will have to do some research. Break down the design task into steps, as on the opposite page:

Design step 1 – the input block

The input will need to gather information on the amount of moisture in the plant. You will need to find a suitable component that will do that.

You will need to use a sensing device, in this case a moisture sensor. You will need to understand how a moisture sensor works before you can proceed.

Once you have the information, from the moisture sensor, on how much moisture is present, that information will be sent to the process block.

Design step 2 – the process block

Your second step will be the process block. This will need to convert the information received from the input into an output you can recognize.

A transistor is a suitable component for this. It is an electronic switch. There are many different types of transistor so you will need to understand how a transistor works before you can proceed.

Design step 3 – the output block

Your final step is the output block. The best way to show when the plant needs watering is for a light to come on. In this case you would use a light emitting diode (LED).

You will need to understand how an LED works before you can proceed.

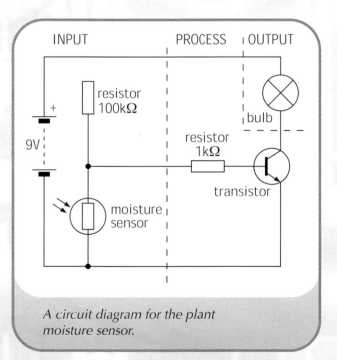

A circuit diagram for the plant moisture sensor.

Design step 4 – putting it together

Once you have understood how all your components work, you can put the system together. This stage is known as creating a **circuit diagram**.

All components have an internationally recognized symbol. These symbols are used in circuit diagrams to show a component – do not use an actual picture of the component.

The circuit diagram should be drawn in a way that makes it easy to see the input process and output components.

Once you have created a circuit diagram for your electronic product, you can begin to develop it and make it.

Development and making

It is important that you test your **circuit diagram** design before you make the final product. If during your research you find an existing circuit diagram that meets your needs, you may wish to use that and modify it to meet your **specifications**.

Prototype circuits

You will need to test your circuit diagram design to discover if it actually works before you make it. Make a **prototype** circuit. If it does not work first time you may have to go back a few steps to find and correct errors. You can prototype circuits using a **bread board** or computer. A bread board allows you to temporarily fix **components** together to make sure the system works. Software such as Crocodile Technology® and Control Studio® enable you to model and test **circuit** design. An example of this is shown below.

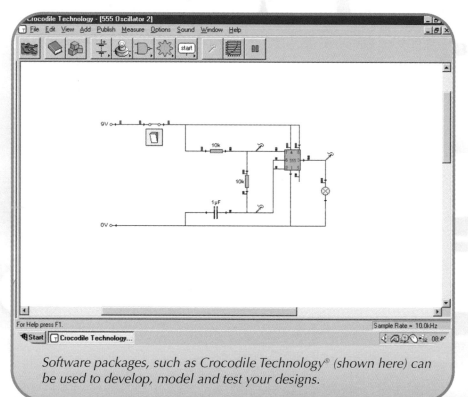

Software packages, such as Crocodile Technology® (shown here) can be used to develop, model and test your designs.

The printed circuit board

When you are happy that the circuit works, you need to design and make a printed circuit board, or PCB.

The PCB design will look different from the circuit diagram in that it is made of a series of tracks, pads and spaces for components to be fitted. A PCB can be designed on computers using CAD software such as PCB Wizard® or Techsoft PCB Design & Make® or it can be drawn by hand or by using transfers.

Making a photosensitive PCB

1 Preparing artwork – Firstly design the required circuit. The best option is to complete the PCB circuit design on a computer and print or plot artwork onto a translucent or transparent film.

2 Expose the PCB to ultraviolet light – Use a **photosensitive** PCB. Remove the protective black plastic from the board to reveal the photo resist. Position the artwork in contact with the photosensitive side of the PCB board. Then place both in a UV exposure unit (lightbox), with the artwork down. Close the lid before setting the UV unit's timer to the correct exposure time.

3 Developing the image – The photo resist is softened by the UV light passing through the transparent areas of the artwork. The developer removes this soft photo resist. Take the exposed board out of the UV unit and place it in the developer. The board should be fully developed in 30–45 seconds.

4 Washing – When the board has been fully developed, remove the board from the developing tank and place it in the spray wash.

5 Etching – The developed and washed board is then placed into an **etching** tank. The lid is closed and the air pump turned on. The etching time will depend on how much background copper has to be etched away. At the normal etching temperature of 45°C, etching should take approximately five minutes.

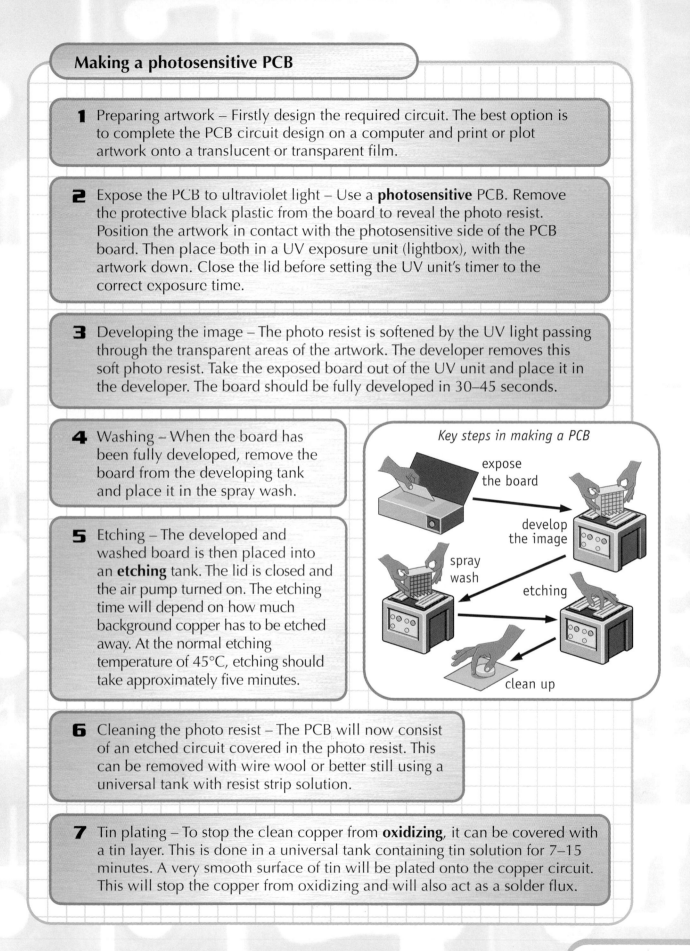

Key steps in making a PCB

expose the board

develop the image

spray wash

etching

clean up

6 Cleaning the photo resist – The PCB will now consist of an etched circuit covered in the photo resist. This can be removed with wire wool or better still using a universal tank with resist strip solution.

7 Tin plating – To stop the clean copper from **oxidizing**, it can be covered with a tin layer. This is done in a universal tank containing tin solution for 7–15 minutes. A very smooth surface of tin will be plated onto the copper circuit. This will stop the copper from oxidizing and will also act as a solder flux.

Evaluation

Evaluation is something you do every day, probably without even realizing it! For example you may be evaluating what shoes to buy or food to eat. Your decision will be based on a number of **criteria**. These are similar to your design **specification**'s criteria (see page 16).

Why do evaluation?

The purpose of evaluation is to improve on what you have done before. Therefore evaluation is a continual process. Throughout the designing, developing and making processes you should keep on evaluating your product and changing it if necessary.

Evaluating can be more interesting and fun if you discuss your products with a friend.

How to do a final evaluation

A final evaluation is a review of your final product. You will need to use your judgement to assess the outcome of the design. Evaluation can be broken down into three sections, each of which is discussed below.

1 Checking your outcomes against the original specification

Read through your original specification. Now decide if you managed to achieve each specification criteria. The specification outlines how you intended your product to turn out, and this may have changed over the course of the design process.

- If you did achieve the specification criteria, for example that the durability is good, you need to say how this has been achieved.

- If you did not manage to achieve a specification criteria, say why it was not achieved, or why it was changed. If changes were made, say how successful they were.

You can write up your assessment of the product as a table like this:

Specification criteria	Question	Answer
Colour: My product will be black and green.	Did the product turn out to be black and green?	No, it was clear that just using black and green did not create the right effect. I changed my design and used a range of colours to much better effect. The result was a much more attractive and marketable design.
Size: My product will be small.	Have you kept the product small?	Yes, I managed to keep the product to a hand-held size although it did turn out larger than I had originally intended. This change in size affected the cost of the product and allowed for more detailed design features.

2 Consumer testing

Consumer testing is getting people who might use the product to test it.

- Find out what they think is good about the product (its strengths), and *why* it is good.
- Find out what they think is poor about the product (its weaknesses) and *how* and *why* the product needs to change.

Write up the consumers' comments in a logical way. You may add comments to support other people's views or comments that argue against their views. (This may help you identify strengths and weaknesses in the product to help you with part 3.)

3 Identifying the strengths and weaknesses of your product

- State what you consider to be the strengths of your product and give reasons.
- Then suggest possible modifications and improvements for the weaknesses you have identified.

Industrial case study: Mega Electronics

Mega Electronics manufactures equipment for **prototype** and small-batch production of printed circuit boards (PCBs), panels and signs. Many of its products are used in schools and other educational establishments.

The bubble etch tank

Traditionally, the most common PCB manufacturing process in schools has been to use a ferric chloride solution in a bubble etch tank, such as that produced by Mega Electronics.

The main advantages of a bubble tank in educational use are:	The main disadvantages of the bubble tank in educational use are:
• familiarity with the system • it is already established in many schools • relatively low cost.	• students cannot see the circuits being **etched** • takes a relatively long time to etch circuits – about 5 minutes • PCBs are immersed in liquid, so boards can be over-etched, removing all the copper • can be a dirty job removing circuits from the ferric chloride tank.

Rotary Jet etcher

Mega Electronics has now developed a new Rotary Jet spray etcher. The company had been selling a rotary etcher for several years. However, this machine was much larger than schools needed, and too expensive for them. So the company re-engineered an existing design into a modern, smaller and more cost-effective product.

The company's Research & Development (R&D) team talked to users of its bubble tanks. The users' views influenced the design of the new etcher, including a new design of board holder, a transparent case so students could see the PCBs being etched, the spray wash system and a lockable reservoir emptying system. It took six months to create a prototype, which was tested in all the company's markets. One result of the field-testing was the development of a different panel or board holder to be used in the metal etching market. This makes the etcher more suitable for use by sign makers and engravers, who want to etch stainless steel and brass nameplates.

Cost was the biggest challenge for Mega Electronics in creating this new product because schools had to be able to afford the Rotary Jet unit. This meant that the development time was relatively long – 18 months in total – but the company now has a far better machine than the older and bigger one.

The main advantages of the new Rotary Jet etcher in educational use are:

- students can see PCBs being etched
- it will etch PCBs about three times faster than a bubble etch tank
- an integral spray wash tank means the whole process is cleaner
- a digital timer controls the etching time and as the board is not immersed in liquid, there is no over-etching after completion
- it allows high-resolution etching with a low failure rate
- it can be used to develop or strip photo resists.

The main disadvantages of the jet etcher in educational use are:

- it is unfamiliar technology for many schools
- the initial cost of purchase is higher.

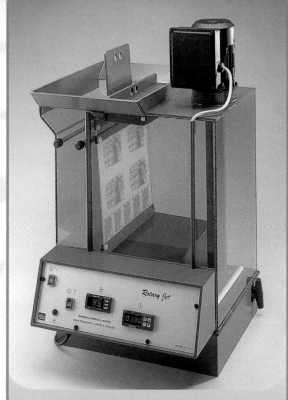

Mega Electronic's Rotary Jet spray etcher.

Using Computer Numerical Control (CNC)

Another way to produce PCBs is to use Computer Aided Manufacture (CAM). Small Computer Numerical Control (**CNC**) **milling** machines like the Suregrave Wizzard DT and the Roland EGX-300 can make PCBs in low quantities.

Alternatively, PCBs can be produced using a photosensitive etching process, then placed into a CNC machine for drilling and cutting out the board to shape.

The advantages of using CNC production in an educational environment are:

- no need to use chemicals to develop and etch circuits
- very accurate and has a low failure rate
- relatively easy to prototype PCBs direct from CAD software, such as Techsoft PCB® Design & Make and PCB Wizard®, without having to create masks
- holes for **components** can be drilled accurately.

The disadvantages of using CNC production in an educational environment are:

- high cost of initial purchase
- can take time to mill very complex **circuits** in large quantities.

Project 1: Map board

The design brief

A small electronic toys manufacturer has asked you to design and make an electronic 'map board' that will light up when the user makes a connection. The board will use five LEDs (light emitting diodes) to highlight five different areas of a picture or image of your choice, using a key.

The finished map board.

Research

You will need to understand the use of the following **components** that are needed to make **circuits** work: light emitting diodes (LEDs) and **resistors**.

Product specification

The product **specification** is a list of things your product must be or do:

- the product will have five LEDs that light up
- the product will not use a PCB
- the product will be made from wood
- the product will use an image of your choice.

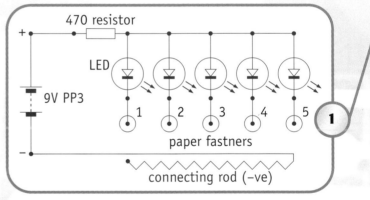

Resources

Materials and components

- 5 mm copper track
- red wire, black wire
- 5 x LEDs (5 mm diameter standard)
- resistor 470R
- 5 x paper fasteners
- PP3 9V battery
- PP3 battery connector
- paper
- **bread board** (for **prototype** circuit)
- 150 x 150 MDF 3 mm thick
- 50 x 50 softwood 12 mm thick
- metal connecting rod

Tools and equipment

- soldering iron
- solder
- wire strippers
- wire cutters
- pillar drill/hand drill
- drill bits (5 mm and 4 mm)
- glue stick
- pencil crayons
- tenon saw
- pen
- PVA glue

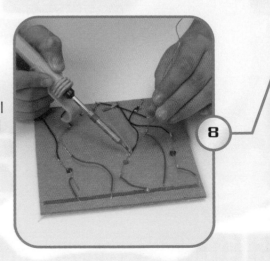

Action plan

Using the following steps as a basis for your action plan for the map board:

Action	Resources	Time needed
1 Design a **circuit diagram** indicating input, process and **output** components	• Pen • Paper • Component symbols	10 mins
2 Collect each of the components identified in the circuit diagram. Place them in a bread board and test the prototype circuit	• Bread board • Components • 9V battery	30 mins
3 Cut the board to shape	• MDF • Tenon saw	20 mins
4 Decorate front of map board with chosen design	• Paper • Pencil crayons • Glue stick	30 mins
5 Drill 5 mm holes for LEDs, drill 4 mm holes for paper fasteners. Fasten these to board	• 5 mm drill bit • 4 mm drill bit • Pillar drill/hand drill	10 mins
6 Use copper track to construct circuit	• 5 mm copper track	10 mins
7 Fix and connect components into circuit	• Components • Wire – red and black • Wire cutters/strippers	10 mins
8 Solder components to copper track and join connecting rod. Add battery and test the circuit board	• Soldering iron • Solder • connecting rod • 9V battery	20 mins
9 Make stand for board	• softwood • PVA glue • Tenon saw	20 mins
10 Test product and make any required modifications	• Product	10 mins

Evaluation

Answer the following questions about your product to help you evaluate how your product development went:

1 How did research help me complete the project?

2 Did I test my circuit design before making it?

3 What was the quality of my soldering like?

4 Did the circuit work first time? If not why?

5 Did the circuit need any corrections?

6 What do other people think of my work?

7 What parts of the project did I find difficult and why?

8 In what ways could I make my product better?

9 Am I pleased with my finished product?

10 Did I enjoy the project?

Project 2:
Steady hand tester

The design brief

Design and manufacture an electronic device that tests how steady your hand is. The product must have an on/off switch and use a **latching circuit**.

Research

Research the following area to help you to develop your product. You should research latching circuits and investigate the use of a thyristor in a latching circuit. You will need to understand the use of the following **components** that are needed to make the **circuit** work: thyristors and **resistors**.

The finished steady hand tester.

Product specification

The product **specification** is a list of things your product must be or do:

- the product must be contained in a wooden box that can be painted any colour
- the toy must be able to be used by children
- the product must use a latching circuit
- the maze must have the start and finish clearly marked.

Resources

Materials and components

- thyristor 2N5060
- resistor 680R
- resistor 470R
- LED
- 1x SPST switch
- 1x PTM switch
- PCB board
- PP3 battery connector
- PP3 9V battery
- softwood

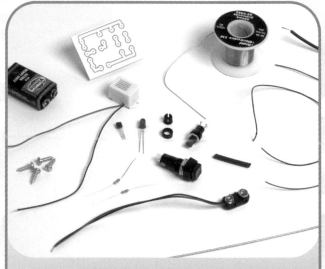

Some of the materials and components used to make the steady hand tester.

- metal brazing rod for probe and maze route
- 6V buzzer
- screws
- 5 mm foamex
- acetate
- hardboard
- black and red wire
- paper
- wood stain

Tools and equipment

- soldering iron
- solder
- wire strippers
- wire cutters
- pillar drill
- drill bit
- screwdriver
- CAD software, e.g., Crocodile Technology®
- UV lightbox and etching tank
- **CNC milling** machine – Wizzard DT or Roland EGX-300
- 1 mm slot drill for CNC
- pen
- printer

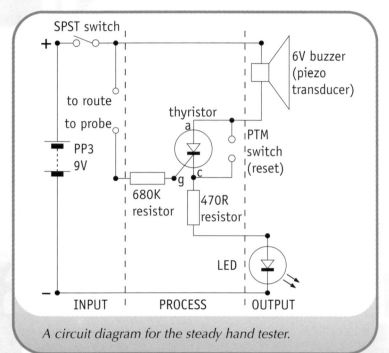

A circuit diagram for the steady hand tester.

Design ideas

1 You need to sketch ideas for the steady hand route for your product.

2 Sketch different ideas for the casing for the product using different shapes, forms and colour. For each idea show:

- how the circuit is intended to fit into the casing
- how the input and **output** components fit onto or into the casing
- how the battery is fitted into the casing.

Action plan

Using the following steps as a basis for your action plan:

Action	Resources	Time needed
1 Design a **circuit diagram** indicating the input, process and output components	• Pen • Paper	20 mins
2 Model the circuit using CAD software	• CAD software	30 mins
3 Design PCB circuit using CAD software, the circuit diagram and your **prototype** circuit. Use a computer program to create the final PCB design	• CAD software • Printer • Acetate	20 mins
4 Make the PCB using an **etching** tank process or CNC manufacture	• PCB transparencies • UV box, etching tank *or* CNC milling machine with 1 mm slot drill • Pillar drill • drill bit	30 mins
5 Solder components to PCB	• Components • Soldering iron • Wire strippers • Wire cutters	1 hour
6 Manufacture the steady hand route using the metal brazing rod	• Soldering iron	20 mins
7 Make sides of box from softwood, top from foamex and base from hardboard	• Tenon saw • Panel pins • Softwood • Foamex • Wood stain • Hardboard • PVA glue	30 mins
8 Solder wire from probe to the PCB and another wire from the PCB to the route. Add a battery and test the circuit board	• Soldering iron • Battery • Solder • Wire • Wire cutters • Probe • Components	30 mins
9 Assemble the product	• Screwdriver • Pillar drill • Screws	30 mins
10 Test product	• Product	10 mins

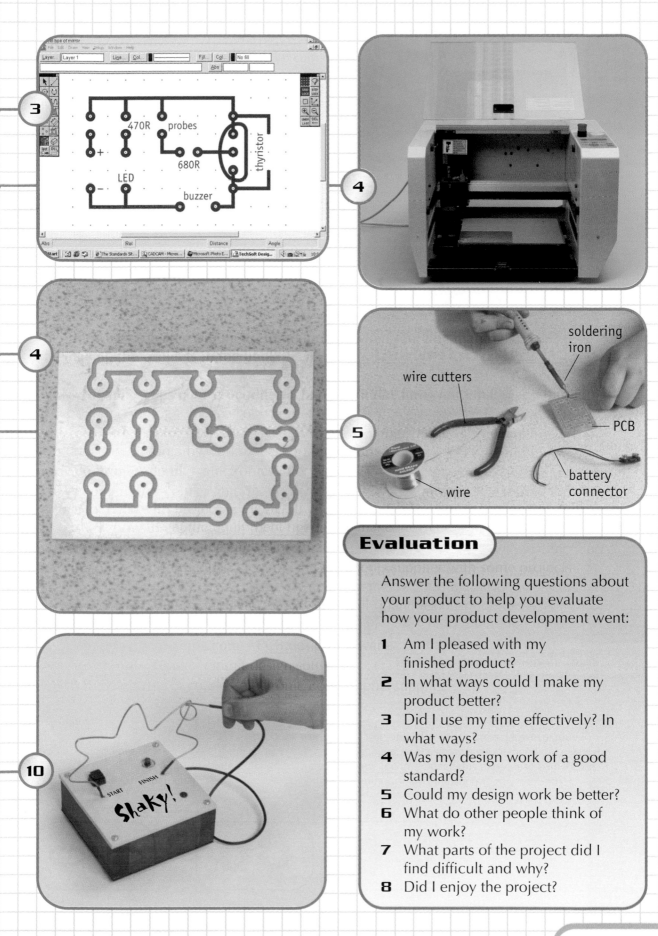

3

470R probes

+

680R

LED −

buzzer

thyristor

4

4

5

soldering iron

wire cutters

PCB

wire

battery connector

10

START FINISH

Shaky!

Evaluation

Answer the following questions about your product to help you evaluate how your product development went:

1 Am I pleased with my finished product?
2 In what ways could I make my product better?
3 Did I use my time effectively? In what ways?
4 Was my design work of a good standard?
5 Could my design work be better?
6 What do other people think of my work?
7 What parts of the project did I find difficult and why?
8 Did I enjoy the project?

Project 3: Buzz box

The design brief

A small electronic toys manufacturer has asked you to design and make a hand-held electronic toy that makes a number of different sounds.

Research

Research the following areas to help you to develop your product. Investigate which types of **integrated circuit (IC)** are able to produce different types of sound. You can find out how the integrated circuit you have selected works by requesting a data sheet from the manufacturer or supplier of the **component**. The data sheet may suggest a sample **circuit diagram** that identifies which other components are needed for the **circuit** to work. It may also suggest ways of using the IC.

You will need to understand the use of other components needed to make the IC work. For the UM3561 sound chip you will need to research:

- how **capacitors** work
- how transistors work
- how **resistors** work.

The finished buzz box.

Product specification

The product **specification** is a list of things your product must be or do:

- the product will produce up to four different sounds
- the product will use a UM3561 sound chip
- the product will be made from Foamex plastic
- a PCB will be needed
- the product will be hand-held
- the product must be safe for users of over five years of age
- the product should withstand regular use
- the product will have an attractive casing.

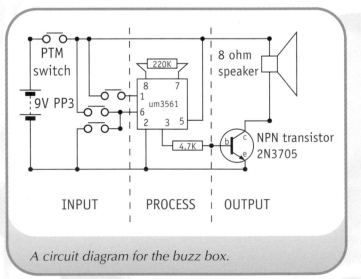

A circuit diagram for the buzz box.

Resources

Materials and components

- sound chip UM3561
- transistor 2N3705
- resistor 220K
- resistor 4.7K
- speaker 8 ohm
- circuit board
- (PTM)
- 4 x push to make switches
- 8 pin DIL socket
- PP3 9V battery
- PP3 battery connector
- Foamex plastic
- PCB transparencies
- **bread board**
- wire

Tools and equipment

- soldering iron
- solder
- wire strippers
- wire cutters
- pillar drill
- drill bit
- CAD software
- **CNC** – Wizzard DT or Roland EGX-300 **milling** machine
- 1 mm and 2 mm slot drill for CNC
- **etching** tank
- UV lightbox
- acetate
- pen
- sticky pads
- line bender
- paper
- printer

Design ideas

Sketch different ideas for the casing for the product, using different shapes, forms and colour. For each idea show:

- how the circuit is intended to fit into the casing
- how the input and output components fit onto or into the casing
- how the battery is fitted into the casing.

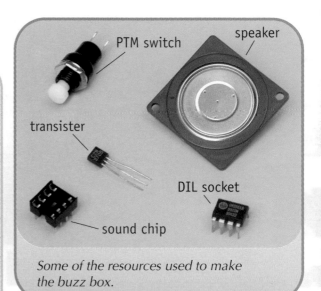

Some of the resources used to make the buzz box.

Hints for success

! Decide whether to make the casing using **vacuum forming** methods, CAD/CAM or by hand.
! Develop a shape for the housing. Curvy shapes are better suited to vacuum forming using High Impact Polystyrene (HIP). More angular shapes are better suited to CAD/CAM or hand methods using wood, Foamex or acrylic.
! The circuit can use up to four sounds. Develop the circuit design to incorporate all four sounds.
! **Prototype** the circuit designs using a bread board.
! Prototype the circuit using software such as Crocodile Clips®, Crocodile Technology® or Control Studio®.

Action plan

Using the following steps as a basis for your action plan for making your own buzz box:

Action	Resources	Time needed
1 Design a circuit diagram indicating input, process and **output** components	• Pen • Paper	20 mins
2 Collect each of the components identified in the circuit diagram. Place them in a bread board and test the prototype circuit	• Bread board • Components • 9V battery	30 mins
3 Design PCB circuit using CAD software, the circuit diagram and your prototype circuit. Use a computer program to create the final PCB design	• CAD software • Printer • Acetate	20 mins
4 Make PCB using an etching tank process or CNC manufacture	• PCB transparencies • UV lightbox, etching tank *or* CNC milling machine with 1 mm slot drill • pillar drill • drill bit	30 mins
5 Solder components to PCB	• Soldering iron • Solder • Components • Wire strippers • Wire cutters	30 mins
6 Make the casing from Foamex using CNC machine	• Foamex • CNC milling machine • 2 mm slot drill • Line bender	30 mins
7 Assemble product	• Product • Sticky pads	5 mins
8 Test product	• Product	10 mins

4

5

6

7

battery connector

Evaluation

Answer the following questions about your product:

1 Am I pleased with my finished product?
2 In what ways could I make my product better?
3 Did I use my time effectively? In what ways?
4 Was my design work of a good standard?
5 Could my design work be better?
6 What do other people think of my work?
7 What parts of the project did I find difficult and why?
8 Did I enjoy the project?

Project 4: Organ

The design brief

A small electronics toy manufacturer has asked you to design and make a hand-held electronic toy that will make music.

Research

Research the following areas to help you to develop your product. Investigate which types of **integrated circuit (IC)** are able to produce musical sounds, or can this circuit be made without an IC?

You will need to understand the use of these **components**:

- slide switches
- **capacitors**
- transistors
- **resistors**
- transducers.

The finished organ.

Product specification

The product **specification** is a list of things your product must be or do:

- the product will produce a range of musical notes
- the product will not use an integrated circuit
- the product casing will be made from Foamex plastic
- the product will use a **CNC**-manufactured PCB
- the product will be hand-held
- the product must be safe for users of over five years of age
- the product should withstand regular use
- the product will have an attractive casing.

Resources

Materials and components

- 2 x transistors BC108
- 1 x resistors 2.2K, 5.6K, 10K, 22K
- 2 x resistors 1K, 3.9K, 4.7K
- 2 x capacitors (metallized polyester 250V 0.1uf)
- piezo buzzer (for converting electrical energy to sound)
- circuit board (PCB)
- on/off switch
- PP3 battery connector
- PP3 9V battery
- Foamex plastic
- wire
- acetate

Tools and equipment

- soldering iron
- solder
- wire strippers
- wire cutters
- line bender
- pillar drill
- drill bit
- CAD software
- CNC **milling** machine – Wizzard DT or Roland EGX-300
- 1 mm slot drill for CNC milling machine
- **etching** tank
- UV lightbox
- pen / paper
- **bread board**
- printer

Design ideas

Sketch different ideas for the casing for the product, using different shapes, forms and colour. For each idea show:

- how the circuit is intended to fit into the casing
- how the input and output components fit onto or into the casing
- how the battery is fitted into the casing.

Hints for success

! Decide whether to make the casing using **vacuum forming** methods, CAD/CAM or by hand.

! Develop a shape for the housing. Curvy shapes are better suited to vacuum forming using High Impact Polystyrene (HIP); more angular shapes are better suited to CAD/CAM or hand methods using wood, Foamex or acrylic.

! The circuit can use BC108 and BC549B transistors or the more modern BC548B ones, which are cheaper and more durable.

! A similar circuit can also be made using a 555 timer IC in place of the transistors.

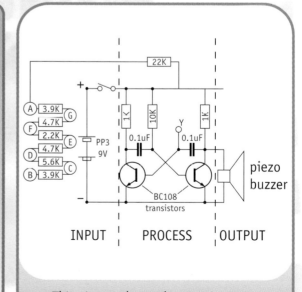

This picture shows the circuit diagram used for the music toy.

Action plan

Using the following steps as the basis for your action plan:

Action	Resources	Time needed
1 Design a **circuit diagram** indicating the input, process and **output** components	• Pen • Paper	30 mins
2 Collect each of the components identified in your circuit diagram. Place them in a bread board and test the **prototype** circuit	• Bread board • Components • 9V battery • Piezo buzzer	30 mins
3 Design PCB circuit using CAD software, the circuit diagram and prototype circuit. Use a computer program to create the final PCB design	• CAD software • Printer • Acetate	30 mins
4 Make PCB using UV box and etching tank process or CNC manufacture	• PCB transparencies • UV lightbox, etching tank *or* CNC milling machine, 1 mm slot drill • pillar drill • drill bit	60 mins
5 Solder components to PCB	• Components • Soldering iron/Solder • Wire strippers/Wire cutters	20 mins
6 Make casing	• Foamex plastic • CNC milling machine with 1 mm slot drill • Line bender	60 mins
7 Assemble product	• Product • Sticky pads	20 mins
8 Test product	• Product	10 mins

2

Evaluation

Answer the following questions about your product to help you evaluate how your product development went:

1 How did research help me complete the project?
2 Did I test my circuit design before making?
3 What was the quality of my soldering like?
4 Did the circuit work first time? If not why?
5 Did the circuit need any corrections?
6 What do other people think of my work?
7 What parts of the project did I find difficult and why?
8 In what ways could I make my product better?
9 Am I pleased with my finished product?
10 Did I enjoy the project?

Project 5: PICBU

The design brief

PICBU is a robot that can be designed to move in any direction. It can also play a tune that you program into it, and has eyes that light up. PICBU is controlled using a peripheral interface controller, or PIC. The **circuit** will power two motors that will allow the product to move in any direction, as well as powering the sound generator and eyes. PICBU is built upon a round base produced using CAD/CAM. The top can be designed individually in whatever style you choose.

Research

Research the following areas to help you to develop your product:

Programmable integrated circuits

This project is going to use software called PIC-Logicator to program the PIC chip. We are going to use the PIC16F627 (use the link to Economatics (Education) Ltd on page 47 to find out more about PIC-Logicator). The diagram for this is shown below.

PICBU!

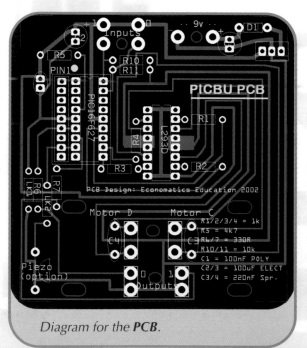

*Diagram for the **PCB**.*

PIC-Logicator

In PIC-Logicator, you create your control system in the form of a **flowsheet**. You drag commands from the command list and place them in cells on the flowsheet working area. You can then use the command's cell detail box to fill in their details as required, and complete the flowsheet by drawing routes to connect the cells. When the **flowsheet** runs, the flow of control follows the route you have drawn, carrying out the command in each cell as it passes through it.

Components

You will need to understand the use of other **components** needed to make the PIC microchip work:

- **capacitors**
- resistors
- transducers

Product specification

The product **specification** is a list of things your product must be or do:

- the product must be driven using two solar motors and a PIC16F627 microchip programmed using PIC-Logicator

- the product can have up to two inputs (sensors) and has two LED outputs and one piezo buzzer. These can be used wherever you feel that they will benefit the product.

- the chassis of the robot is going to be made out of Foamex and manufactured using a Roland EGX-300 **CNC milling** machine. The dimensions and manufacturing data for the chassis are shown in the picture on the right.

- the PICBU must play a tune at some point during its routine

- the circuit that is going to be used is shown below:

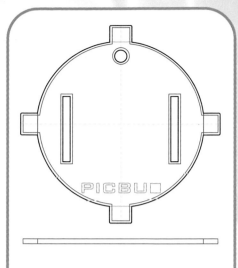

- [ ] Tool Path 2mm tool 3mm depth
- [ ] Detail drawing
- [ ] Tool Path 2mm tool 1.5mm depth
- [ ] Tool Path 1mm tool 0.5mm depth
- [ ] Tool Path 1mm tool 3mm depth

Material: 3mm Foamex

The dimensions and manufacturing data for the chassis of PICBU.

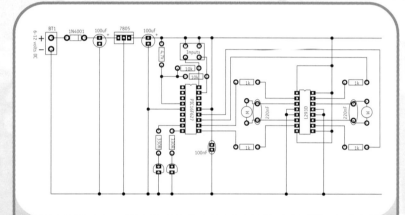

The circuit diagram for PICBU. You can find this and other information on the Economatics website (see page 47).

Resources

Materials and components

- PIC microchip PIC16F627
- L293D motor controller chip
- 4 x resistor 1K
- resistor 4.7K
- piezo buzzer
- PCB
- 2 x push to make switches
- 18 pin DIL socket
- 2 x solar motors
- capacitor 100nF
- 2 x capacitor 100uF
- diode 1N4001
- voltage regulator 7805 vr
- 2 x resistor 330R
- 2 x resistor Link 0R
- PP3 battery connector
- 9V PP3 battery
- Foamex plastic chassis and wheels
- sticky-backed tape
- velcro pads
- wire

Tools and equipment

- PIC-Logicator with programmer
- soldering iron
- solder
- wire strippers
- wire cutters
- cutting board
- knife

Hints for success

! A good idea for the casing is to use a pre-manufactured component, such as a margarine tub or small bowl. You could decorate it using a range of materials and colours.

! The flowsheet should integrate a tune using the sound command and two outputs. Keep the flowsheet as simple as possible, and test it thoroughly before downloading it onto a PIC microchip.

Action plan

Using the following steps as a basis for your action plan for making PICBU:

Action	Resources	Time needed
1 Design a flowsheet using PIC-Logicator	• PIC-Logicator	3 hours
2 Manufacture the circuit board using CAD/CAM or use a pre-manufactured board	• CNC milling machine • PCB	20 mins
3 Solder the circuit board using the diagram on page 41	• Soldering iron • Solder • Components • Wire strippers • Wire cutters	2 hours
4 Manufacture the casing	• As design dictates	2 hours
5 Download flowsheet into PIC microchip using PIC programmer	• PIC-Logicator and PIC programmer • PIC chip	30 mins
6 Assemble product	• Foamex plastic chassis and wheels • Sticky-backed tape • Velcro pads • Cutting board and knife	30 mins
7 Test product	• PICBU	10 mins

Evaluation

Answer the following questions about your product to help you evaluate how your product development went:

1. Am I pleased with my finished product?
2. In what ways could I make my product better?
3. Did I use my time effectively? In what ways?
4. Was my design work of a good standard?
5. Could my design work be better?
6. What do other people think of my work?
7. What parts of the project did I find difficult and why?
8. Did I enjoy the project?

Electronic components chart

Component	Specification	Size	Cost
Battery	Zinc chloride PP3	9V	£0.50 ($A1.32)
Battery cell	Alkaline button cell	1.5V, 6.8 mm diameter	£0.10 ($A0.26)
Battery connector	Heavy duty	PP3	£0.10 ($A0.26)
Capacitor	Radial electrolytic	10V 100u	£0.05 ($A0.13)
CNC PCB	SRBP	100 mm x 60 mm	£0.50 ($A1.32)
PTM switch	Push to make switch	small	£0.13 ($A0.34)
DIL socket	8 pin	Pitch 0.3	0.04 ($A0.10)

Component	Specification	Size	Cost
Electronic buzzer	PCB mounted	6V	£0.65 ($A1.72)
IC	Sound generator chip	UM3561	£0.50 ($A1.32)
Photo etch PCB	FR4 Epoxy glass	100 mm x 60 mm	£2.25 ($A6.00)
Resistor	Carbon film	0.25 ohm	£0.01 ($A0.03)
Standard LED	30 mA 80 lum	5 mm diameter	£0.05 ($A0.13)
Transistor	Silicon NPN	BC548B	£0.07 ($A0.18)
Ultra slim speaker	8 ohm 70db	30 mm diameter	£0.50 ($A1.32)
Wire	Stranded	0.2–100 m reel	£2.45 ($A6.50)

Glossary

amplifier device which uses power from another source to increase the overall power

analysis examine something in detail, think about it in order to learn from it

atom smallest units of matter that can take part in a chemical reaction

bread board block which allows you to temporarily fix components to it to make sure a circuit works

capacitor component that stores charge

circuit electrical network that has at least one closed path for the flow of a current

circuit diagram diagram showing how an electrical current will pass through a circuit

CNC Computer Numeric Control

components different parts of a product, such as an integrated circuit

conductive material/conductor material which allows the flow of electricity through it

consumer anybody who buys or uses a product

criteria various standards set on which you can make a judgement about something

current flow of electricity

design brief statement which describes the problem that the product design needs to solve

electron one of the particles that make up an atom. It has a negative electric charge.

electromotive force (EMF) amount of energy, measured in volts, required to produce a flow of electricity.

etching process of removing unwanted material from a printed circuit board (PCB)

evaluation/evaluating process of comparing the finished product with the specification

fine etch crystals granule-like substance mixed with water to formulate chemical liquid for etching

flowsheet series of linked boxes that show the order of making something or a control system

fluctuating varying in an irregular way

ICT Information Computer Technology (also known as Information Communication Technology)

insulating material material which does not allow electricity to flow through it

integrated circuit (IC) minute piece of silicon containing thousands of components connected together by aluminium strips

laminated thin layer of covering over something

latched/latching circuit type of circuit that remains on after a process has been carried out

milling cutting and shaping

modelling using a computer to generate products or making small-scale ideas

negative power rail zero volts or ground rail

neutron particle with the same mass as a proton, but with no electrical charge

Ohm's law mathematical equation showing the relationship between voltage, current and resistance in an electrical current

output giving out information or making something happen

oxidizing creating oxygen

photosensitive sensitive to or changed by light

piezo-electric transducer transducer that uses the principle of piezo-electric effect. Piezo-electricity is when some crystals, for example, quartz, obtain opposite electrical charges on opposing faces when put under pressure. It is used in generating ultrasonic waves.

programmable integrated circuit (PIC) small chip that accepts programs to be downloaded on to it to control a system

proton one of the particles that make up an atom. It has a positive electric charge.

prototype full version of a product, used for pre-production testing

resistor component that reduces the flow of current through the part of the circuit
        to which it is connected

rosin yellowish solid resin

silicon very common non-metal used in many products, including glass

solid state signal passes through a switch and leaves the circuit in one state or the other

specification set of criteria that a finished product or final solution must achieve

systems approach breaking down the design process into easy parts

vacuum forming method of moulding plastics over a shape called a former. The plastic is heated
        until soft, then sucked over a hard former.

Resources

The following websites will be useful to look at when sourcing materials and making the projects in the book:

www.crocodile-clips.com/crocodile/technology/index.htm – information on Crocodile Technology® design software

www.designtechnology.org.uk – website created by the authors; dedicated to D&T education. It contains worksheets and project ideas.

www.doctronics.co.uk – electronics information

www.economatics.co.uk – information on PIC-Logicator software. You should look at this for help with Project 5: PICBU. If you look in the Education section you will find out how to get the equipment needed to make PICBU.

www.madlab.org – contains circuit information

www.maplineducation.com – electronic components supplier with some projects to make for students

www.mecelex.co.uk – manufactures PCBs in small quantities

www.megauk.com – electronics equipment supplier

www.new-wave-concepts.com – PCB design software

www.quickroute.co.uk – circuit design software

www.rapidelectronics.co.uk – electronic components supplier

Index